Noah, Build Your Boat

Old Testament Stories & Pictures by Kids

Edited by Jeff Kunkel

"Great is the Lord and greatly to be praised..."
Psalm 48:1

"The desert in Israel."
—Andrew Larson, age 9

**In loving memory
of Paul Bernard Hessert,
My Father in the Faith**

"God and Moses meet on the Holy Mountain
with lots of lightning, thunder, smoke, and fire."
—Tessa Morris, age 10

NOAH, BUILD YOUR BOAT
Old Testament Stories & Pictures by Kids

Copyright © 2002 Jeff Kunkel
All rights reserved. Except for brief quotations in critical articles or reviews, no part of this book may be reproduced in any manner without prior written permission from the publisher. Write to: Permissions, Augsburg Fortress, Box 1209, Minneapolis, MN 55440.

Scripture passages are from the New Revised Standard Version of the Bible, copyright © 1946, 1952, 1971, 1989 by the Division of Christian Education of the National Council of the Churches of Christ in the USA. Used by permission.

Cover and book design by Michelle L. N. Cook

ISBN 0-8066-4402-8

The paper used in this publication meets the minimum requirements of American National Standard for Information Sciences—Permanence of Paper for Printed Library Materials, ANSI Z329.48-1984. ♾™

Manufactured in Singapore   AF 9-4402

06   05   04   03   02   1   2   3   4   5   6   7   8   9   10

Contents

Introduction	6
The Very Beginning (Genesis 1:1-31)	8
The Garden of Eden (Genesis 2:4-10, 15-24)	10
Noah, Build Your Boat (Genesis 6—9)	12
Sarah & the Mystery Men (Genesis 12:1-5; 17:1-5; 18:1-15)	14
She Looked Back (Genesis 19:1-2, 12-17, 23-26)	16
Birth of Jacob & Esau (Genesis 25:19-26)	18
Don't Be Scared (Genesis 28:1-3, 10-19)	20
Moses Meets God (Exodus 2:11-15; 3:1-20)	22
Moses' Great Plan (Exodus 12:21-28)	24
Crossing the Red Sea (Exodus 14:5-26)	26
Creating a Holy Nation (Exodus 19:1-20; 20:1-17)	28
The Z Man's Daughters (Numbers 27:1-7)	30
A Love Story (Ruth 1:1-22; 2:1-11; 4:1-8, 13-16)	32
The Truth-Teller (I Samuel 3:1-11, 13-19)	34
David's Great Fight (I Samuel 17; 20; 26; 37)	36
Life into Grief (Job 1:1-21)	38
Isaiah Sees the Lord (Isaiah 6:1-13)	40
Daniel in the Lion's Den (Daniel 6:1-27)	42
A Big Fish Story (Jonah 1:1-2; 3:1-10; 4:1-11)	44
A Prayer (Psalm 23)	46
Writers and Artists	48

Introduction

Five thousand years ago, people already lived in the deserts and mountains along the Mediterranean Sea. These people gathered into tribes, and each tribe became like a nation, with its own language, beliefs, laws, and customs. Most of these tribes believed there were many gods who ruled the heavens and earth, but twelve tribes believed that only one God created and ruled the heavens and earth. These twleve tribes spoke the Hebrew language and came to call themselves "Israel," a Hebrew word that means "God rules."

The people of Israel, later known as Jews, told stories about how and why God created and ruled the heavens and earth, and how God loved the people of Israel in a special way. In addition to telling stories about God, they created laws and customs that showed their love and respect for God. These stories, laws, and customs were written down and became the Hebrew Scriptures, the sacred writings of the Jews.

Thousands of years later, Jesus was born in this same desert area along the Mediterranean Sea in Bethlehem, a village near the city of Jerusalem. As a Jewish boy, Jesus learned the Hebrew Scriptures and came to know and love the God of Israel. Jesus had many followers who believed that he was the Son of God and the promised Messiah, or Christ. After Jesus died, his followers—Christians—wrote stories about his life and created their own scriptures, now known as the Bible. Christians included the Hebrew Scriptures, which they called the Old Testament, in their

"This is a picture of Jeff Kunkel.
We call him, 'Mr. K.'"
—Zachary Garmen, age 7

Bible. They included stories about Jesus in the part of the Bible that they called the New Testament. You can find out more about Jesus in my book, *Jesus, This Is Your Life: Stories & Pictures by Kids*.

The first Old Testament story that I learned as a boy was about Noah, the last good man left on the earth, and how God used Noah to create a new world. The story featured animals, a huge boat, a great storm, the first rainbow, and a promise from God. I loved this story! Over the years, I have reread and studied the story of Noah and the flood—and many other exciting tales from the Old Testament. I have shared these stories with children from different areas, races, and backgrounds.

Here's how I shared the stories: First, I gathered a group of kids and read them a "juicy" Old Testament story, a story with plenty to see, smell, hear, taste, and touch. Then, I put a bunch of art supplies in front of the kids and invited them to rewrite the story in their own words and draw or paint the story. All the stories and pictures in this book have been created by these children—ages 5 to 12. Their names and ages are listed, along with the Bible reference for each story, so that you can also read the story in the Bible. The kids' stories and pictures are fresh, brave, and true—and they're sure to make you laugh, frown, wonder, trust, and learn. Enjoy!

Jeff Kunkel

Jeff Kunkel

"And a little child shall lead them."
—Old Testament book of Isaiah, 11:6

The Very Beginning

The Old Testament begins with this story, the creation story.

Genesis 1:1-31
written by Christopher Ledford, age 11

In the very beginning, there was only pitch black darkness. God said, "Let there be light." He named the light "Day" and the darkness "Night." He was pleased.
On the second day, God said, "Let there be a dome," which he called "Sky." He put water in the sky and called it "Rain." On the third day, God said, "Let there be land," which he called "Earth," and "Let there be water on the land," which he called "Sea." On the fourth day, God said, "Let there be lights in the sky," and God called the nighttime lights "Stars," and the daytime light "Sun."
On the fifth day, God said, "Let there be plants that have grains and fruit," and "Let there be birds and sea monsters and all kinds of animals, wild, small, and large—lions and tigers and bears, oh my!" On the sixth day, God finally got around to people and said, "Let there be human beings so that they can name the animals and take care of the earth." It took God six days to make all this because he had to figure out where to put everything.
On the seventh day, God looked at everything he had made and was pleased, and he took a break because he was tired after using all his powers.

"These are the first flowers, which God made. My mom grows all of them in her garden now except the one on the right, which is very rare."
—Kayla Huetteman, age 6

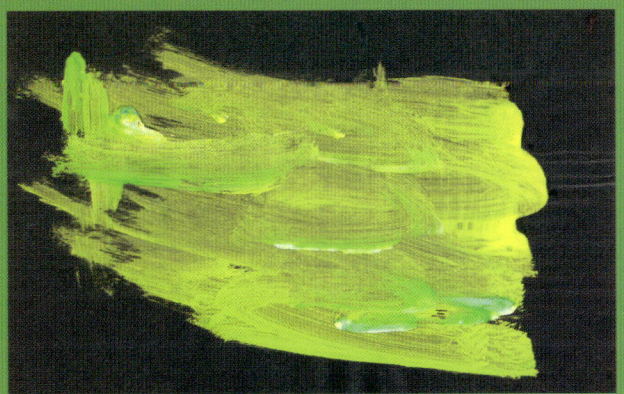

"God made light."
—Tyler Niles, age 9

"God made sky."
—Gia Paoli, age 12

"God made land and sea."
—Tyler Niles, age 9

"God made sun, moon, and stars."
—Khaela Moya Hiramatsu, age 7

"God made plants, birds, and animals."
—Nicky Reed, age 8

"God made people."
—Tyler Niles, age 9

The Garden of Eden

This was the first home of human beings.

Genesis 2:4-10, 15-24
written by Kelly Reed, age 10

When God created the world, he wanted someone to live on it and take care of it. So God made a man and put him in a beautiful garden filled with tulips, daisies, roses, rabbits, and a magical tree. He told the man to take good care of the garden but to stay away from the magical tree.

God named the man "Adam," and he named the garden "Eden." Adam worked hard in the garden all day, but when he came home, he wanted somebody to talk to, so God put him into a deep sleep, and took a bone out of his body. Ouch! God used that bone to make a woman, someone Adam could talk to. Her name was Eve.

Adam and Eve worked together in the garden, pulling weeds, planting flowers, and cleaning up. At night, they talked a lot. One day they saw some beautiful apples on the magical tree. Yum! They each took a bite of an apple. God heard them munching and said, "You two are eating apples from the magical tree!"

"No we aren't," they said.

"You have disobeyed me and lied, so now you must leave the Garden of Eden and find another place to live."

The End.

"The Garden of Eden has an apple tree and fish pond."
—Lauren Tullis, age 6

"This is Adam and Eve holding hands. They live in the Garden of Eden, which has a fence around it."
—Kayla Huetteman, age 6

Noah, Build Your Boat

God used Noah, a boat, a flood, and a rainbow to start the world over.

Genesis 6–9
written by LeeDell Thomas, age 10

There was a wise old man named Noah. He had no faults and was close to God, but other people were far from God. One day, God told Noah to build a boat that was 450 feet long, 75 feet wide, and 45 feet high. Noah didn't even ask God, "What am I going to do with such a big boat?" He just built it.

When Noah was done, God told him to fill his boat with live animals, a male and female of every kind. Noah didn't even say, "What happens when all those animals start to fight and stink up the boat?" He just did it. When Noah was done, God said, "Now get in your boat and stay there."

God sent a great rainstorm that lasted for forty days and nights and flooded the whole world. But Noah, his family, and all the animals stayed warm and dry in their boat, which floated on top of the waters, going up and down with the waves.

When the rains stopped and the waters went down, Noah sent out a dove to check for dry land. When the dove came back with an olive branch in its mouth, Noah knew that there was dry land again and it was almost time to start a new world. God put a rainbow in the sky and said, "A rainbow is my promise that I will never again destroy the world by flood."

Noah said, "Amen."

"Noah's boat in the storm."
—Lee Washington, age 5

"The flood has gone down, the rainbow has arrived, and Noah's boat is again resting on dry land."
—Katie Reutter, age 10

Sarah & the Mystery Men

Abraham and Sarah are the father and mother of all the Hebrew people.

Genesis 12:1-5; 17:1-5; 18:1-15
written by Amy Bischoff, age 9

When Abraham was ninety-nine years old, he saw God, and God said, "I am the Almighty, the Lord. If you obey me and do what is right, I will give you many children." Abraham fell to the ground and started to laugh. This must be a joke, he thought. My wife is ninety years old. We're both way too old to have babies!

A couple of days later, three mystery men walked past Abraham's tent, and Abraham invited them to dinner. Sarah cooked, and all the men ate dinner under a tree near the tent. One of the mystery men asked, "Where is Sarah?"

Abraham said, "She's in the tent."

Another mystery man said, "In nine months, we will come back, and Sarah will give birth to a baby." Sarah heard this and just laughed.

One of the mystery men said, "I heard Sarah laughing!"

Sarah got scared, stopped laughing, and said, "No. I didn't laugh."

"Yes, you did," said another mystery man.

Nine months later, Sarah had a baby, just like the mystery men had told them. Abraham and Sarah named their baby "Isaac," which means "laughter!"

Sometimes we laugh at God's promises, but they come true!

"Old woman Sarah just heard that she will have a baby, so she is laughing and going to her tent."
—Amira Essuman-Mensah, age 7

"The three mystery men visit Abraham and Sarah."
—Amy Bischoff, age 9

She Looked Back

Lot was Abraham's nephew, and he lived with his family in a city full of evil people.

Genesis 19:1-2, 12-17, 23-26
written by Tyler Niles, age 9

The Lord heard that two great cities, Sodom and Gomorrah, were full of people who had turned away from him and were doing bad things. So God sent two angels to destroy the cities. At the city gate, the angels met a good man named Lot, and he said to them, "You two can stay at my house." Lot did not know that the two visitors were angels.

Early the next morning, the angels said to Lot, "Wake up! The Lord is about to destroy this city!"

Surprised, Lot asked, "How do you know this?"

"Because we are angels!" they said. "If you want to be spared, take your wife and daughters and get out of this city. Quick!"

The angels led Lot and his family to the edge of the city and said, "Now run for your lives and don't ever look back!"

Suddenly, the Lord rained burning sulphur on the cities of Sodom and Gomorrah, but Lot's wife looked back at the city. When she did, God changed her into a rock of salt, and she had to stare at the wrecked city forever.

"The angels meet Lot at the city gate of Sodom."
—Robbie Ferguson, age 8

"Lot's wife before and after."
—Diane Bischoff, age 12

"Sodom and Gomorrah before and after."
—Diane Bischoff, age 12

Birth of Jacob & Esau

Jacob and Esau were twin boys born to Isaac and Rebekah, but only one of them would receive Isaac's blessing.

Genesis 25:19-26
written by Tyler Niles, age 9

Sarah died when she was 127 years old, and Abraham died when he was 175 years old. Isaac, their son, lived on, and he married a woman named Rebekah. But they had no children. Isaac prayed to the Lord for a child, and Rebekah became pregnant with twins. Even before the twins were born, they fought inside of Rebekah, which she did not like one bit. She asked the Lord, "Why do these two fight within me?"

The Lord said, "The one who is born first will get his father's blessing, so they are both trying to be born first!"

Finally Rebekah gave birth, and she had twin boys. The first one had reddish-pink skin and a hairy body. His name was Esau, and because he was born first, he got Isaac's blessing. The second one was born holding tight to Esau's heel. His name was Jacob. The brothers fought like cats and dogs.

"The twins, Jacob and Esau."
—Claire Bowie, age 6

"Jacob and Esau (the red one) are fighting before they are born!"
—Karissa Carson, age 11

Don't Be Scared

Jacob tricked Isaac, took the blessing away from Esau, and ran for his life.

Genesis 28:1-3, 10-19
written by Audrey Huetteman, age 8

Jacob was going on a trip to get away from his brother, so he packed his bags and rode off on his donkey. When he got tired, he got off his donkey, set up camp, and picked some grass to sleep on. But he used a stone as his pillow.

That night, as he slept, he dreamed that he saw a long, long ladder going from earth to heaven and that angels were climbing up and down the ladder. A voice said to him, "Jacob, I will give you a nice home and your kids will be strong and healthy."

Jacob woke up scared and asked, "Who are you?"

"I am God, the God of Abraham and Isaac. Don't be scared."

"At the top of the ladder to heaven is a beautiful gate with pink flowers growing on it."
—Audrey Huetteman, age 8

"This is Jacob on the ladder,
which goes up and down between heaven and earth."
—Kayla Huetteman, age 6

Moses Meets God

The Egyptians made the Hebrews into slaves, and God helped them get free.

Exodus 2:11-15; 3:1-20
written by Nicky Reed, age 8

One day, Moses was wandering around the Holy Mountain looking for his sheep and goats. Moses didn't find them, but he saw flames up ahead and found a bush on fire. What a strange bush, he thought. It is on fire but not burning up! When the Lord saw that Moses was coming closer, he called out to Moses from the middle of the bush and said, "Moses! Moses!"

Moses answered, "Yes, here I am."

God said, "Do not come any closer. Take off your sandals. You are standing on holy ground. I am the God of Israel."

Moses put his hands over his face because he was afraid to look at God.

God said, "I have heard the cries of the people of Israel. They live in Egypt, and the Egyptians treat them like dirt. I want you to bring them out of Egypt to a land where they can be free."

Moses said, "But, God, I am no leader. I am a nobody!"

God said, "Don't worry! I'm going to make you into a leader! Trust me!"

"The burning bush."
—Kennedy Solomon, age 12

"Moses discovers the burning bush in a cave on Mt. Sinai, the Holy Mountain."
—Christine Ledford, age 12

Moses' Great Plan

This story created the Hebrew holy days called "Passover," which are still celebrated by Jews all over the world.

Exodus 12:21-28
written by Hannah Leigh Burnett, age 8

This is a story about a man named Moses who saved the Hebrew people from the Angel of Death. One day, Moses told the Hebrews, "The Lord is going to punish the Egyptians for treating us so bad. He is going to send the Angel of Death to kill every firstborn baby boy. Here's what you have to do to make sure that the Angel of Death passes over your house. Select a lamb or baby goat to kill and spread its blood across and down both ways of your doorpost. That way, when the Angel of Death comes to take your family, he will think that they were already taken, and he will pass over your house."

So the Angel of Death visited all the Egyptian homes and took away their baby boys, but the Angel of Death did not visit the Hebrew homes or take even one Hebrew baby.

"The Angel of Death, with hair made out of lightning."
—Hannah Leigh Burnett, age 8

"The yellow castle belongs to the ruler of Egypt, Pharaoh. He is shouting, 'No!' because he sees that the Angel of Death has taken his firstborn baby. The brown houses belong to the Israelites, who have covered their doorposts with blood to keep away the Angel of Death."
—Mishea Hasty, age 12

Crossing the Red Sea

Moses led the Hebrews out of slavery in Egypt, but their troubles did not end.

Exodus 14:5-26
written by Erika Guisina, age 12

Moses helped the people of Israel escape from Egypt, which made the Egyptians mad. So the Egyptians got on their horses and went after the Israelites. When the Israelites saw the Egyptians coming, they got mad at Moses and said, "Why did you bring us here? It would have been better to live as slaves in Egypt than to die out here in the desert!"

Moses said, "Lord, help us! Now or never!"

The Lord said to Moses, "Lift up your walking stick and hold it over the sea. The waters will part, and you and your people will be able to walk across on dry land."

Moses did as the Lord said. A mighty wind blew and parted the waters, and the people of Israel walked to safety on dry land between two walls of water. When the Egyptians followed, Moses lifted his walking stick again, and the water fell back and drowned the Egyptians and their horses.

God can make life, but he can take life, too.

"Moses is on the left. He is carrying his walking stick and shouting, 'Let my people go!' at the Pharaoh of Egypt."
—Tyler Niles, age 9

"The Israelites have just crossed the Red Sea safely, but now the Egyptians are trying to follow on horseback, but the sea will swallow them. Behind them are the Great Pyramids of Egypt, which are still standing."
—Christine Ledford, age 12

Creating a Holy Nation

God wanted a nation that would obey and love him.

Exodus 19:1-20; 20:1-17
written by Skye Wilson, age 12

Three months after the people of Israel escaped from Egypt, they camped at the foot of Mt. Sinai, the Holy Mountain, and Moses went up the mountain to speak with God. God told him, "I have delivered you from Egypt and brought you here. If you obey and love me, I will make you and your people a holy nation."

Moses told this to his people. They said, "Yes, we want to be a holy nation, obeying and loving God."

Moses said, "God will tell us how to be holy—get ready to meet him."

On the third day, thunder, lightning, and a thick, black cloud came over the mountain, followed by a trumpet blast. The Israelites trembled with fear and didn't want to get any closer to God, but Moses went up the mountain so that God could speak to him.

God said:
1. Worship me only and no other gods.
2. Do not bow down to any statue or idol.
3. Do not use my name for evil purposes.
4. Rest on the seventh day, the Sabbath.
5. Respect your father and mother.
6. Do not kill anyone.
7. Do not have sex with anyone other than your husband or wife.
8. Do not steal.
9. Do not lie about someone else.
10. Do not desire what belongs to someone else.

Moses came back down and told the people, "The Lord has not come to hurt you, but to show you what is right."

"Moses on top of Mt. Sinai, ready to talk to God."
—Christopher Aiken-Forderer, age 9

"Israelites are at the foot of the Holy Mountain.
They are afraid to meet God."
—Justin Stern, age 8

The Z Man's Daughters

In Old Testament times, women could not inherit money, name, or property. But five sisters changed that.

**Numbers 27:1-7
written by Katie Reutter, age 10**

Once upon a time, there was a man named Zelophehad, but since no one could pronounce his name, he was called the Z Man. The Z Man had zero sons and five daughters. Their names were Mahlah, Noah, Hoglah, Milcah, and Tirzan.

One day, the Z Man died, so someone had to inherit his property and name, but in those days, only sons could do that. The Z Man's daughters thought this was very unfair, so they went to find their leader, Moses. They found him in a tent, dressed in an elegant blue and white robe and surrounded by a big crowd of people. The daughters said, "Our father died, and he had no sons, but we wish to inherit his property and his name."

Moses said, "This is an unusual request, but I will present it to the Lord." The Lord agreed to their request, so the daughters got to keep their father's property and name, which made them happy.

"This is one of the Z Man's daughters. She's happy because God is good to her."
—Tatiana Moadang, age 5

"These are the Z Man's daughters."
—Tanas Sliheet, age 8

A Love Story

The book of Ruth is about love, family, and surprises.

Ruth 1:1-22; 2:1-11; 4:1-8, 13-16
written by Katie Reutter, age 10

Once, long before Israel had a king, the crops in Israel failed, and the people ran out of food. A man named Elimelech and his wife, Naomi, took their two sons out of Israel so that they could live in Moab, a place with better crops and more food. Elimelech died in Moab, and Naomi was left alone there with her sons, who married Moab girls, Ruth and Orpah. But then her sons died, too.

Naomi heard that the Lord was blessing Israel with good crops again, so she got together with Orpah and Ruth and said, "I am going back to Israel, but you two will have a better life here in Moab. And if you're lucky, you'll marry again."

Orpah and Ruth started crying and said, "No! No! We want to go with you."

Naomi said, "Hush, now, and do as I say."

Orpah decided to stay, but Ruth said, "I will go with you, and your people will become my people, and your God, my God." And with that, Naomi did not say another word.

Once they were back in Israel, Ruth and Naomi began to gather food from a rich man's field. The rich man's servants told the rich man, Boaz, that Ruth and Naomi were taking his food. Boaz went out to his field to chase away Ruth and Naomi, but he fell in love with Ruth and married her.

"Ruth is crying because she doesn't want Naomi to go without her."
—Jenna Nibert, age 8

"This is Elimelech, Ruth, and their sons. The whole family left Israel and walked to Moab to find food. They are all sad because they miss Israel."
—Nicky Reed, age 8

The Truth-Teller

As a boy, Samuel listened to God; so God made him a truth-teller, a prophet.

I Samuel 3:1-11, 13-19
written by Audrey Huetteman, age 8

The boy Samuel lived in the temple with his teacher, Eli. One night, Samuel woke up and heard a voice say, "Samuel! Samuel!"

Samuel said, "Yes, sir." He ran to Eli and said, "You called me, and here I am."

Eli sat up in bed and said, "I didn't call you. Go back to bed."

The next night, Samuel heard the voice again. The boy didn't know that the voice belonged to God, so he got up, ran to Eli, and said, "You called, and here I am."

Eli said, "I didn't call you. Go back to bed."

The third night, God called Samuel again, and the boy got up and ran to Eli.

Eli said, "I did not call you. But somebody called you, that's for sure, and I bet it was God. If he calls you again, say, 'Speak, Lord, my ears are wide open.'"

So Samuel went back to bed. God spoke again. "Samuel! Samuel!"

"Yes, Lord. My ears are wide open," Samuel answered.

God said, "Eli has spoken evil against me, so I will do something terrible to him."

The next morning, Eli asked Samuel, "What did the Lord say?" And Samuel told him.

"He is the Lord," Eli said. "He will do whatever is best."

"Samuel woke up to the sound of God's voice coming in through the window."
—Robbie Ferguson, age 8

"Samuel is in bed inside the temple, and God's voice is breaking in."
—Emma Lambert, age 8

David's Great Fight

David, a shepherd boy, becomes Israel's greatest king.

I Samuel 17; 20; 26; 37
written by Ben Reutter, age 8

Once there were two armies, the Israelites and the Philistines. They faced each other across a valley, ready to fight. The Philistines had a giant, whose name was Goliath. He was nine feet tall, mean, and ugly. Goliath came out and yelled, "Send someone to fight me. If he wins and kills me, my whole army will be your slaves. But if I win and kill him, your whole army will be our slaves. Who will fight me?"

No one answered. The next day, a shepherd named David visited his brothers who were soldiers in the Israelite army. Then Goliath yelled again, "Who will fight me?"

David said, "I will fight him."

Saul, leader of the Israelite army, said, "You can't fight him. You're a shepherd boy."

David said, "I may be a shepherd, but if a lion or bear attacks my sheep, I kill it with my slingshot. The Lord has saved me from lions and bears. He will save me from a giant!"

Goliath laughed at David. "You're just a boy! I will feed your body to the animals!"

David said, "I don't think so. You have a spear, a shield, and a helmet, but I have the Lord God Almighty!" David slung a stone at Goliath. The stone hit him in the forehead, broke his skull, and he fell face down onto the ground–kaboom!–dead as dead can get!

All the Philistines ran away.

"This is David's slingshot shooting a stone at the giant, Goliath. There are five smooth stones left for battle."
—Adam Warmoth, age 7

"Goliath and little David meet in a valley for battle."
—Rebecca Muller, age 8

Life into Grief

Job was a man who had everything—and lost it all.

Job 1:1-21
written by Helen Williams, age 9

The Lord and Satan were talking in heaven, and the Lord asked, "What have you been doing lately, Satan?"

Satan answered, "Walking on the earth, looking around."

"Did you see my faithful servant Job?" asked God.

"Yes," Satan replied, "But he didn't impress me."

"Why not?" asked God.

"He might be praising you now, God," Satan answered, "but that's because you've given him everything—children, camels, sheep, houses, servants, and money coming out of his ears. I bet if Job had all that taken away from him, he would stop praising you and curse you instead!"

"I'll take your bet, Satan," God said. "Go ahead and take away all Job has, but don't hurt him."

So Job had everything he loved taken from him. In grief, he shaved his head, tore his shirt, and said, "I came with nothing, and I'll die with nothing. Praise God!"

Job did not curse God, so Satan lost the bet.

"Job"
—Dan Duncan, age 10

"Lightning bolts strike Job's sheep and turn them into fried furballs."
—Sarah Warmoth, age 9

Isaiah Sees the Lord

Isaiah, a priest in the temple, tells how he became a prophet.

Isaiah 6:1-13
written by Alysandre Saavedra, age 8

In the year King Uzziah died, I saw the Lord. He sat upon his throne, and his cloak filled the temple. There were little fiery creatures all around him. Each had six wings. With two they covered their mouths, with two they covered their bodies, and with two they flew. They called to each other:

"Holy, holy, holy! The Lord Almighty is holy!" Their words shook the temple, and the temple filled with smoke.

I said, "I am doomed! For every word that comes out of my mouth is sinful, and every word that comes out of my people's mouths is sinful, too."

Then one of the fiery creatures flew down to me. He held up a big, burning coal with tongs and touched it to my lips. The fiery creature said, "Your sins are forgiven. You will speak now of holy things."

Then I heard the voice of the Lord asking, "Who will carry our message? Whom can we send?"

"Send me," I said.

"The temple altar with burning coals."
—Dan Duncan, age 10

"The temple, with God on his throne, the red, six-winged seraphim holding a burning coal, and Isaiah with his arms in the air."
—Katie Reutter, age 10

Daniel in the Lion's Den

*Daniel was kidnapped, taken far from home,
and put to work as a servant for a Babylonian king.*

Daniel 6:1-27
written by Sophia Hanson-Richter, age 6

There was a man named Daniel. He worked for the king and did such a good job that the king put him in charge. The other men who worked for the king did not like this and wanted to get rid of Daniel. They knew that Daniel prayed only to God, so they went to the king with a law that read, "For the next thirty days, everyone has to pray to the king or they will get thrown in the lion's den." The king signed the law.

Daniel kept praying to God and did not pray to the king. So the men told the king, "Daniel is praying to God, not you! You must throw him into the lion's den!"

The king liked Daniel and did not want the lions to eat him, but he had signed the law and that was that. So the king threw Daniel into the lion's den.

The rest of that day, the king did not eat or drink because he was worried about Daniel. That night, the king prayed to Daniel's God and did not sleep a wink. In the morning, the king went to the lion's den and shouted, "Daniel, are you okay?"

Daniel answered, "I am still alive. God sent an angel to shut the mouths of the lions."

This is how the king learned that God was greater than any king on earth.

"One of the lions with its mouth shut by an angel."
—Lauren Horst, age 7

"The lions are all around Daniel, but God's angel is keeping him safe."
—Kelsey Chappell, age 7

A Big Fish Story

God asked Jonah to tell the truth to the people of Nineveh.

Jonah 1:1-2; 3:1-10; 4:1-11
written by Ingmar Prokop, age 12

Once upon a time, there was a man named Jonah. He was a Hebrew, and God told him to go to the city of Nineveh and tell the people to be nicer to the Hebrews. Now, poor old Jonah didn't like the Ninevites, so he went to Joppa to escape the Lord. In Joppa, he boarded a ship and set sail. The Lord saw this, got angry, and sent a storm to sink the ship. The ship's crew decided that Jonah was the cause of the storm and threw him overboard, which stopped the storm. The Lord had cooled down a little, so he didn't want Jonah to die and sent a big fish to swallow Jonah and keep him safe.

Jonah stayed in the belly of the big fish for three days and three nights, praying to the Lord that he might be let out onto dry land. The Lord heard his prayers, and the big fish vomited Jonah onto a beach. Then, for the second time, God asked if Jonah would go to Nineveh, and this time Jonah said, "Yes."

Jonah went to Nineveh and said, "All people are equal in the eyes of the Lord, so you Ninevites better be nicer to the Hebrews!" The Ninevites said, "Okay." But Jonah still did not like them and went out into the desert to pout, and God made a plant grow over him to give him shade.

"God asked Jonah to go to Nineveh, but Jonah got mad and refused to go."
—Jenna Nibert, age 8

"Jonah is inside the belly of the big fish, which swallowed him."
—Annie Ryan, age 12

A Prayer

The Book of Psalms is a collection of poems, prayers, and songs.

Psalm 23

The Lord is the shepherd of all the sheep.
He gives us a big feast.
God loves everyone.
I can't accept all the blessings—it's too much!
God guards us from evil because he loves us.
The shepherd takes us to a new place even better than the old place.
All I can say is, "Thanks!"

written by Katie Kobashigawa, age 8

God is like my mother, sweet and kind.
God is like my father, leading me to water when I need it.
God is like a shepherd, keeping me safe in the dark.
God gives me the food I need at supper, and that's all I need to live.
God takes me to fields to run around in.
I make my shelter out of the trees.

written by Elise Scripps, age 11

"This is the cup of life. God fills it to overflowing."
—Emma Drysdale, age 10

"The Lord is a shepherd of sheep and people, taking care of us all."
—Julie Huggins, age 10

Writers and Artists

Katie Reutter, age 10, Walnut Creek, California, cover, 13, 30, 32, 41
Kiley Tonsing, age 5, Walnut Creek, California, back cover
Andrew Larson, age 9, Modesto, California, 3
Tessa Morris, age 10, Los Altos, California, 4
Zachary Garmen, age 7, Walnut Creek, California, 6
Christopher Ledford, age 11, Oakland, California, 8
Kayla Huetteman, age 6, Oakland, California, 8, 11, 21
Tyler Niles, age 9, Oakland, California, 9, 16, 18, 26
Gia Paoli, age 12, Oakland, California, 9
Khaela Moya Hiramatsu, age 7, San Ramon, California, 9
Nicky Reed, age 8, Alameda, California, 9, 22, 33
Kelly Reed, age 10, Alameda, California, 10
Lauren Tullis, age 6, San Rafael, California, 10
LeeDell Thomas, age 10, Pittsburg, California, 12
Lee Washington, age 5, Pittsburg, California, 12
Amy Bischoff, age 9, Wheeling, Illinois, 14, 15
Amira Essuman-Mensah, age 7, Walnut Creek, California, 14
Robbie Ferguson, age 8, Crystal Lake, Illinois, 16, 34
Diane Bischoff, age 12, Wheeling, Illinois, 17
Claire Bowie, age 6, Los Altos, California, 18
Karissa Carson, age 11, Sunnyvale, California, 19
Audrey Huetteman, age 8, Oakland, California, 20, 34
Kennedy Solomon, age 12, Oakland, California, 22
Christine Ledford, age 12, Oakland, California, 23, 27
Hannah Leigh Burnett, age 8, Dublin, California, 24
Mishea Hasty, age 12, Oakland, California, 25
Erika Guisina, age 12, Columbia, South Carolina, 26
Skye Wilson, age 12, Los Altos, California, 28
Christopher Aiken-Forderer, age 9, Los Altos, California, 28
Justin Stern, age 8, Los Altos, California, 29
Tatiana Moadang, age 5, Los Altos, California, 30
Tanas Sliheet, age 8, Oakland, California, 31
Jenna Nibert, age 8, Pleasanton, California, 32, 44
Emma Lambert, age 8, Crystal Lake, Illinois, 35
Ben Reutter, age 8, Walnut Creek, California, 36
Adam Warmoth, age 7, Los Altos, California, 36
Rebecca Muller, age 8, Los Altos, California, 37

Helen Williams, age 9, Los Altos, California, 38
Dan Duncan, age 10, El Cerrito, California, 38, 40
Sarah Warmoth, age 9, Los Altos, California, 39
Alysandre Saavedra, age 8, San Jose, California, 40
Sophia Hanson-Richter, age 6, Alameda, California, 42
Lauren Horst, age 7, Oakland, California, 42
Kelsey Chappell, age 7, Oakland, California, 43
Ingmar Prokop, age 12, Palo Alto, California, 44
Annie Ryan, age 12, Palo Alto, California, 45
Katie Kobashigawa, age 8, Los Altos, California, 46
Elise Scripps, age 11, Los Altos, California, 46
Emma Drysdale, age 10, Los Altos, California, 46
Julie Huggins, age 10, Los Altos, California, 47
Austin Bowie, age 7, Los Altos, California, 48

"Jacob and Esau are still inside their mommy, but they are already fighting."
—Austin Bowie, age 7